FUN POEMS

FUN POEMS

From Uncle Bernie

A BERNIE BARNES

ILLUSTRATOR, MARILYNN A. CONNER

iUniverse LLC
Bloomington

FUN POEMS
FROM UNCLE BERNIE

iUniverse books may be ordered through booksellers or by contacting:

iUniverse LLC
1663 Liberty Drive
Bloomington, IN 47403
www.iuniverse.com
1-800-Authors (1-800-288-4677)

ISBN: 978-1-4759-9520-6 (sc)
ISBN: 978-1-4759-9522-0 (ebk)

Printed in the United States of America

iUniverse rev. date: 07/12/2013

DEDICATION

In memory of Margaret Ann Tripp Barnes
And to:
Children;
    Mark William and Cynthia McGraw Barnes,
Jack Douglas Barnes, Lori Ann and Stanley Fox,
and Kirk Mathiasen Barnes.

Grandchildren:
    Christoph Samuel, Alexander David, and Jefferey Elliott
Barnes, Kari Ann Fox Bacino and husband Kristopher Brian
Bacino, Bradley Richard and Lisa Joanne Adams Fox, and
Daniel Brent Fox.

Great Grandchildren:
    Caleb Michael Bacino and Hallie Ann Bacino.

ACKNOWLEDGEMENTS

(As with many statements, it's not possible to list all who helped without leaving out some special ones, but there has to be a stopping point somewhere.)

Marilynn Conner for graphics, Peter Baca, for technical help, Sarah Crews for literary support, Ralph Rittenhouse for reviews, Sally Vella for her critique, Kate Sexton for her promotions, Jane and Paul Rudd for marketing, and many, many boosters: Kay Anderson, Monica Abdul, Nasir Khan, Judy Kimball, Eric Ford, Ronna Jermain, Chris McClintock, Charlotte Craven, Steven Mora, Jeff Cassel, Mary Tener, Joan Brown, Mary Marsh, Joe Lubin, Ron Hinz.

BIOGRAPHY

A Bernie Barnes is a writer and author of poetry books and novels after a varied career in engineering, industrial and consumer sales and marketing. He is a graduate of the University of Nebraska, a veteran of U. S. Navy as seaman in World War II and commissioned officer in the U.S. Naval Reserve, retired. His is an inventor, scientist, former CEO and corporation manager. He enjoys service to the community and church. Other activities include cooking, gathering with friends and family, and part time businesses.

As author, his books are:
Scope of Life
Fun Poems
Dreams and Love
The Birth of Christmas Mountain
Life and Spirit Lyrics

DESCRIPTION

Our purpose is bring to everyone the fun, joy and enrichment of life in the form of entertaining and insightful verse. It is hoped that each one will be encouraged and celebrate life as they enjoy the fun and successes depicted in these poems for inspiration, pleasure and enjoyment.

FUN POEMS, PART 1

TABLE OF CONTENTS

GIRAFFE WITH BROKEN NECK

I saw a strange sight, a crooked neck giraffe,
How it survived, I can't explain to you;
Visitors would come to stare and to laugh,
When they saw him in his pen at the zoo.

He could eat and drink, just like his brothers,
And see out of the corners of his eyes.
He'd frolic and play the same as others,
Though his famous neck was a shorter size.

The bent necked giraffe is an example,
How to push any handicap of ours,
Aside and do whatever we're able,
To enjoy the journeys in our life's hours.

SPEED DEMON

Side streets and byways, he spurns,
Taking circles and u-turns,
Past flying chicks and old mares,
At high speed on town thoroughfares,

A slow moving wooden cart,
Loaded with a ladder part,
Stopped ahead and blocked the road,
But, he just ducked under the load.

We know he may reap the wind,
And reckless speeds cause his end;
We hope he sets better pace,
For self control will win the race.

CAN YOU BOUNCE
A WOODEN BALL?

Once, I had a little red ball,
All made out of wood;
When I bounced it on the wall,
It fell down with a thud!

My friend said, "I'll bounce it for you,
Up and down all day;
Tomorrow, I'll show you, too!"
But, I said, "There's no way!"

To my surprise, the next morning,
He had it in tow.
His trick was to add a string
And that made a Yo-Yo!

Now, I'll always remember,
You can change hard things;
When problems you encounter,
The answers may be "strings"!

ARTIST'S KNIFE

He peeled an apple round and round,
An artist's skill I thought profound.
Carefully cut from core to core,
The skin spiraled down to the floor.

My grandfather said not a word
As I sat by the cutting board
And learned by quiet example
To correctly pare an apple.

I keep two lessons from that day;
Some haven't seen an artist's way,
And we remember examples;
For telling can't peel the apples.

THE ZOO

Open the big iron gates wide,
Welcome all the children inside.

The penguin is smaller,
The giraffe is taller,

The hippo gargles,
And the tiger snarls

Elephants sound,
And lions are loud.

Monkeys play,
Donkeys bray,

Laugh of hyenas,
Won't slow the cheetahs.

Polar bears swim,
Peacocks are prim,

Camels slobber and spit,
And zebras, seem quiet.

Give these a home, with others too,
Adding people makes it a zoo!

UNINVITED FRIEND

Spider, spider, on the wall,
Why did you leave your garden?
Spider, spider, hear my call,
Don't spin your web in the den.

Spider, spider, on the wall,
Please, don't crawl upon my bed.
Spider, spider, hear my call,
Eat your meal of flies instead!

Spider, spider, on the wall,
You may live as a recluse;
Spider, spider, hear my call,
To live with me is no use!

Spider, spider, on the wall,
Vital to Nature, I know;
Spider, spider, hear my call,
But, just say goodby and go!

MISTER KOKO'S YOYO

Talented Mister Koko,
With his cool yellow yoyo,
Did tricks like the "waterfall"
And "walk-the-dog", I recall.

Children cheered Mister Koko
And his spinning string yoyo,
When seeing up behind him,
A "cradle" or "pendulum".

I watched skilled Mister Koko
And that fun twirling yoyo,
So, I could go practicing,
To copy his artful swing.

Success of Mister Koko,
Was, I learned from my yoyo,
Practice each day from sun-up
And never, never give up.

JOY OF JOURNEY

A journey cannot be prime
Unit of life experience,
For it is comprised of time,
And a place where one exists.

A journey's pause can reveal
Its direction and progress,
As well as faults you conceal
And chance at time-space success.

A journey means naught, unless
You will reflect its purpose,
Or scheme of consequences
And destination you chose.

It's not in the traveling
You find enjoyments measure;
But, like a ship in sailing,
Reaching port is the pleasure.

"WINGO"

"Wingo" was his nickname.
For his left arm was lame,
And used as brace lever
'Gainst his other member
When handling newspapers.

He stood the corner well,
Though cold rain or snow fell
Or came hotter weather.
There's no one could better
His vending of papers.

One day dawned, unforeseen
When that gray, corner scene
Was now without Wingo;
And his loud 'cheerio'
When he passed the papers.

Now appears image sad
Of empty concrete pad.
Void of noise and bustle
And each morning's hustle,
When it's time for papers.

Wingo salutes again,
His left arm without pain,
On a corner, golden.
He stands whole, in Heaven,
Without his newspapers.

WIN AND LOSE

As one, the whole house held its breath,
To win or lose, was on the line;
It could be end of sudden death,
The last-second shot was airborne.

The short arc ball failed to go in
And the crowd yelled a mighty groan.
Though saddened by what might have been,
The losers knew the margin thin!

Already thinking next season,
Sang; "wait 'til next year", with a grin.
The winners grasped the lucky win,
And took the trophy home again.

WOBBLY WOBBLE

A Wobbly Wobble rolled around,
Climbed up a ladder and fell down;
Never saw that Wobble before,
So couldn't tell if he was sore.

Wobbly Wobble was now grounded,
Badly hurt, his crying sounded,
His foot swelled uo like a balloon.
Doctor said, "he shouldn't walk soon".

Since then, sits in a big soft chair
And can't go and wobble anywhere;
He'll lose that name Wobbly Wobble,
And might be called, "Double Trouble"

If you're sure-footed and can run,
You won't wobble in racing fun;
But, to be careful and not slip,
You must always watch where you step.

THE GOOD NAME

Some reflect on their inherited name,
And seek to preserve its reputation;
To honor and enhance personal fame,
In respect for their ancestors station.

But, others, because of avarice and greed,
Seek selfish ends without moral compass.
Lack of guide or sense of another's need,
Leads to their good name covered with tarnish.

Day after day, we must make right choices;
Self assured to gain life that's trustworthy,
We'll hear not the rabble-rouser voices,
For clear conscience is character glory.

THE FISH

I waded in the swampy river,
A wily catfish I hoped to find.
Cold air and rain caused me to shiver,
But, only that fish was on my mind.

I named him Houdini for his art
And talent of escaping, you see,
But I had persistence, on my part,
To try once again for victory.

In a few tries, my hook had him caught,
I think he knew I was back again.
The fray lasted longer than it aught,
In each turn, he was playing his game.

He turned to dive into a deep hole
Near the overhanging willow tree.
There, the line caught, so I lost my pole,
And saved me the need to set him free.

LESSON AT ELEVEN

My Daddy said,
"Don't climb on the roof,
I do not spoof;
You'll fall and hit your head there."

Tonight I dread,
When at Dad's woof,
He sees the roof;
I wish I'd never gone there.

"I see," he said,
"The burden of proof
Is on the roof;
You left a great big scratch there."

I sure caught Ned!
Now, I'm no goof;
I'll leave that roof
Forever, and alone, there!

SPACERY RHYME

I saw a little space ship
Flying up in the air.
It flew into my window
And hid behind a chair.

A bright green light was shining
As I stood beside it.
But, when the hatch was opened,
No one was inside it.

As I was looking, looking
To find how it got here,
Suddenly, before my eyes,
I saw it disappear!

I wonder, was what I saw
God's angel watching me?
Or, perhaps, it was a dream,
What d'you think it could be?

DOG GONE

I lost my dog along the trail,
That led to the town of Monroe.
Out of my pickup, he just bailed
And ran out across the meadow.

He is black with a long white tail,
If you see him. please let me know,
He'll get in trouble without fail;
Every mail truck, he will follow.

I must find him by tomorrow
Before he tears somebody's mail.
I'll take him home and give him chow,
Then, watch him wag his long white tail,

ANIMAL TRAITS

There are things animals can teach us;
The cat shows us how to stretch muscles,
And the cow shows how chewing prevails;
The horse has mastered his rests and paces,
And the sheep follow their leader's trails.
Pigs show us how to get enough sleep,
And chickens watch all pecking details.
Now owls are sober, so quiet keep;
Monkeys are playful, family bunch,
And our dog's eye begs without a peep;
But, those pesky parrots talk too much!

SEAWAY'S TOLL

Like an untamed animal,
Moving swift and wild,
Cold ocean can turn on all,
Who, by her, are beguiled.

Life tolls pay for sea's larder,
Men must give the price.
Sadly, she gives no quarter,
Demanding storms embrace.

'Tis the ancient story,
Men who love the seas;
Brave sailors through history,
Were lost beneath the waves.

SECRET GOLD

The treasure map, rolled up tight,
Was hidden away, somewhere.
A thin tube placed out of sight,
Only the captain and Pegleg knew where.

High seas tossed their ship around
And storm clouds menaced the crew.
Winds nearly ran them aground,
But, the map was safe, old Pegleg knew.

Ten fathoms high, rose the wave
Fast swamping the schooner down.
Most were lost to the ship's grave,
But, the captain and Pegleg were found.

The story of pirates gold,
Buried and lost to the past,
Is one mystery oft told
Where Pegleg retired to town, at last.

The captain now lifts a toast
To the hard life of the sea
With Pegleg as the rich host,
And his gold pegleg for all to see.

FAR-OUT IMAGE

In my "dream" of real life, there;
I cannot see the world aright.
For one side is another,
Visions swapped to confuse me
And right is left, left is right.
The hair parts on the other side,
Backward is my lapel pin:
Quirky image, in my mirror.

SHIPPIN' OUT TO SEA

Shippin' out to sea, my dear,
I'm shippin' out to sea,

I can no longer stay here,
I'm shippin' out to sea.

The old salt spray beckons me
To adventurous lands across the sea;
I'm shippin' out to sea.

Sunlight guides the ships that ply
Through green-white water beneath the sky;
I'm shippin' out to sea.

In Westward sky, sea gulls glide,
Adding to my longing aches inside;
I'm shippin' out to sea.

Please pack my bag, shirts and socks,
I can't live, any more, on these rocks;
I'm shippin' out to sea.

Shippin' out to sea, my dear,
I'm shippin' out to sea.

I can no longer stay here,
I'm shippin' out to sea.

NEVER GIVE UP

Comments by all when they heard,
Little steer went job hunting,
"Won't amount to much", said Bird,
"He is a deformed runt thing."

"He'll not grow big", said the Horse
Cow said, "He's got but one horn".
Pig said, "Handicapped, of course,
Right from the time he was born."

When Rodeo fair came to town,
And hired 'One Horn' as the best,
He became bull of renown,
And famous throughout the West.

Children, there's those who say no
To world good you want to do,
Or help others where you go;
Doing what's right, that's for you.

SOL

The sun sustains all living things
Yet, it's one of smallest stars of all
In the universe's stretch of galaxies.
Though we are fed and nourished from it,
We seldom wonder how it came to be.

Man stands in awe of it's radiant power;
Evolution has no answer or clue
To this miracle of nuclear fusion,
Because it could not have formed by itself
And science says it was made out of nothing.

Old Sol's rays makes the oxygen we breathe,
Using the vegetation all around;
Continues to build carbon blocks of life.
So we can have rain for crops and our thirst,
It vaporizes water and lifts it high.

Look in hydrogen and helium atoms
And you see spaces and vast emptiness.
States the evolutionist's religion:
The sun came to exist by destiny;
But, only God is source of creation.

WAYSIDE LIFE GOES ON

What is more noticeable
Than a lion on the green?
And what is more fast changing,
Than its growing feathering
Of gossamer parachutes?
Which are released to the wind,
To seed more generations
Of yellow dandy flowers.

STEADY FOX

The fox's ears detects each sound
To tell enemies from prey.
In shadows, sees all around,
The creatures who shun the day.

He will act, as standing by,
But, decoys his position;
For his ancient name is sly
And he stays on his mission.

We count him as an ally,
His sharp nose can smell a rat.
He tames his ecology
And rules his vast habitat.

The fox remains a symbol,
For diligence and duty.
He stands alert and able;
Steady, throughout history.

POWER

My green eye is open
As it shines in the room,
But yet, I am asleep;
Now, quiet is the boom.

I like the mode I'm in,
The P S doesn't peep;
But when the switch is on
It growls to life, zip-zeep.

Slowly colors splash on,
Going from gray to bright;
And the horrors do flash,
All captured in it's light.

A green eye open wide,
I am the sleep-mode light.
Power, asleep inside,
'Til ready to be bright.

SUN SAILING

To sail to the moon on future flights,
Just climb aboard your ion ship;
There, guided by red laser lights,
You set your speed for a half-day trip.

Force beams power your launch into space
And lock onto our satellite,
The solar winds setting the pace
For orbiting loop just overnight.

Your trip to the silver orb over,
Set blast off to be homeward bound.
You may want to be a space rover;
As for me, I will stay on the ground!

WATCH THE TINY WORLD

I saw a teeny spider crawling on my wall,
The size of a dot, I didn't believe my eyes.
What could be the use of such an insect so small?
And that set me thinking of world made micro size.

There must be tiny mites and animals to eat,
Little and wee, human eyes cannot even see.
The very cobweb that spider sets to complete
Appears as some dust on the floor to such as we.

But, to that eight-legged spider out in the yard,
Grasses look like trees; sand, like boulders all around.
So, beware little children and be on your guard;
You'll find miniature creatures crawling on the ground.

WILD ANIMALS

There was a cool rabbit,
Scooting around my shop
And, as was his habit,
Ran away with a hop,
When he saw me turn up.

Next, I saw a squirrel,
Not the least bit skittish,
Swishing his bushy tail;
Staying on to finish
Eating nuts he relished.

A bird perched in a tree,
Became wild and noisy;
And when he spotted me,
Flew circles crazily,
Scolding me thoroughly.

Most animals are wild
And so cannot be tamed;
Some dogs and cats are mild,
But, since they bite the same,
Careful, I'll will remain.

CULTURE

I used to have a TV
That could turn itself off.
In the midst of a story,
It would begin to cough!

At first, it faded, and then
Completely disappeared!
Left with only words and wind,
The stories were very weird.

Nothing to do was a pox,
So bored, I nearly cried;
Then, I found a little box
With knobs along the side.

I dusted the thing I found,
And squealed with delight;
For out of that box of brown
Came music in the night!

"It's my girlhood radio,
Liked to hear," said Mommy,
"Opera, Hit-Parade Show,
Little Orphan Annie."

I'm glad the video broke!
For in songs, books and friends,
I've found life's not a mere joke,
Nor just what TV sends!

AN HOUR OF QUIET HUMMING DAY

A box,
A pile of rocks,
Busy, picking-up fingers;
An hour of quiet humming day,
This is a happy child at play.

A stove,
Some pans and bowls,
Floury, rolling-pin fingers;
An hour of quiet humming day,
This is a cook in a cake way.

A phone,
Paper and pen,
Doodling, tap-tapping fingers;
An hour of quiet humming day,
This is a woman at her say.

A spread,
Chicken and bread,
Licking, pick-pickle fingers;
An hour of quiet humming day,
This is family's picnic in May.

A bed,
'Neath foot and head,
Folding, sheep-counting fingers;
An hour of quiet humming day,
This is a man at nap to lay.

A life,
A love and strife,
Building, task-doing fingers;
An hour of quiet humming day,
This is but a moment we stay.

A blow,
A storm and snow,
Soothing, prayer-held fingers;
An hour of quiet humming day,
This is how troubles melt away.

TO JUMP OR NOT TO JUMP

Riding a cow,
Seems absurd, somehow.

I am glad I,
Didn't give a try.

Though tempted to,
Brains told me not do.

To break a bone,
Sure's to be what's done;

And, so then, down
Climbed I, from the barn!

ROMAN NUMERALS ARE PICTURES

Numerals, Romans did make,
Strange numbers in ancient days;
Each little stick like a stake,
Combined in different ways.

To make a "one" in Roman;
Put a cap on top up high,
Then, a base on the bottom
Makes it like a capital "I"   I

Here's how the numbers are done:
To make Roman number "two"   II
Put a "one" beside a "one";
Add "one", that's three for you.
                                                      III

A four is "V" minus "one",
As "V" is for five, you see;   IV
Now, the minus "one" is done
Putting the "one" in front of "V".   V

"Six", of course" is opposite:
A five with "one" more added.   VI
For a "seven" and an "eight"   VII
Add "one" or a "two", to the end.
                                                      VIII

You think it looks like a fence?
That's right, and too long of lines;
So they made those Roman "tens"
With a "X", but, what of "nines"?

X

You have guessed the "nine", I'll bet!
It's just little "X" for "ten"
With a "one" put before it;   IX
But, after, makes "eleven".

If you did study Latin   XI
In Roman time long ago,
You would write; "L", "C", "D", "M",
But, the math is hard, you know!!

UNCROWNED COWBOY

I fell in rodeo ring,
A steer horn gash in my side.

Bleeding from my punctured lung,
I'm scratched from the bronco ride

And, the Cowboy Hall of Fame.

GOD'S SKY DIVER

A loon soared to a point high,
Then dove straight down in the night;
Downward swoop with mournful cry,
Echoing through diving flight.

Partly veiled in near darkness,
Sky diving with dirge-like sound,
Marked strange habit of nature's
Bird of flight, gravity bound.

I'm awed by loon's innate moves,
And wonder at its story;
For I know that God approves
All His creation's glory.

CAPTURED

In the wild life of ranching,
Of a worth without measure,
Is the horse, its great treasure,

A horse comes with attached strings,
Like back breaking bales of hay,
Feeding and cleaning each day.

Curry combing and rubbings;
Rewarded in grateful eyes
And contented mumbling sighs.

Making demeanor gentling;
You begin to see of course,
How magnetic is my horse;

He captures me each morning.

LOOKING DOWN TO LOOK UP

Now look down, under the grass,
To worlds below our feet;
Where busy creatures do pass
In tiny, vast realms beneath.

There, in soils of the ground;
Teeming, moving, bacteria,
Insects, and worms do abound
In worlds so miniature.

Unnoticed by those above
And also unknown to me;
A universe some do love
And man microscopes to see.

There, the amazing life flows
In seas of enzymes and germs,
Helping the macro world to grow;
Mysteries we've yet to learn.

Look again, under the grass
To worlds below our feet,
Where busy creatures do pass
In tiny, vast realms beneath.

I HEARD A WHISTLE

I heard a whistle, not far away,
Sounding much like a flute at play,
Melodic and pleasant to my ear,
Floating on the soft evening air.

I sat to listen 'til twilight's end.
When silence came, I was saddened,
For I'd lost what I might not regain,
Rare joy I can't again obtain.

I heard a whistle, not far away,
Sounding much like a flute at play,
Melodic and pleasant to my ear,
Floating on the soft evening air.

LIFE: NORTH BY WEST

Amid the land of the Dane,
Of farms and fish, sun and rain;
Stands an island in the sea,
Set North in antiquity.

Came to Stor Viby village
A sturdy maid of young age,
From Midskov to tend small ones;
And in her stay, met Math's son.

His name was Niels, hers Kari;
As love grew, they would marry.
This tale turned more romantic;
They wed 'cross the Atlantic!

The year; Eighteen Sixty Nine.
The couple; forebears of mine,
Great Grandparents came to give
America for me to live.

Thus, from the land of the North
To the West came roots of worth;
Pioneers in this new land;
My heritage, great and grand.

This is the story of Niels and Karoline (or Caroline)
Mathiasen, who embarked from Isle of Fyn,
Denmark and were married in Omaha, Nebraska
on June 11, 1870.

THE HAND IS FASTER

One hand sets up a distraction,
While the other hides a secret.
Yes, we know there's a transaction
That fools eyes, but, we can't see it.

It's the art of the magician.
He practices each slight movement
'Til he can make things disappear,
For our awe and entertainment.

Magicians live to ripe old age,
For they make us think time stands still.
These sly trick masters of the stage
We'd like to be, but, never will.

WILD, WILD WOLF

Wild is his name,
Wild, wild animal.

No one can tame
The ever wild wolf.

Stalking his game,
The lurking lone wolf.

Fierce is his fame;
Running in the pack.

No one can tame,
He is wild, wild wolf.

THE GAME OF LIFE

You gotta face the pitch
That life hurls hard and fast,
You need to get that hit
Before the ball sails past.
Whether it's the sweet spot
Or swing's a little late,
You gotta grab the bat
And step up to the plate.

The hit into center
Brings forth the joyful shout,
But the third errant strike
Gets the sad call; "you're out".
'Tis then, you must rally
And not be second-rate,
You gotta grab the bat
And step up to the plate.

You play out the innings,
More failures than success;
Striving toward a win
'Til maybe yanked in six.
If the Manager plays you
So the ninth is your fate,
You gotta grab the bat
And step up to the plate.

FORCE 7 MONSTER

I stepped to a spot of lighted circle,
From glow of storm damaged streetlight bezel;
I strained to move against the gale force wind,
So I could exam the cut on my shin.
The dangling broken globe swayed to and fro,
Flashing eerie sparks like fireworks in snow,
A gust of wind lifted my hat to flight,
Into the vast darkness of stormy night,
On Beaufort scale, gauged a force seven wind,
With that much power, one can barely stand.
Then, I realized the wind strength was growing,
With more force than I remembered knowing.

Frantically, I searched for some shelter,
A ditch or wall to shield me from weather,
I followed the railroad bank in the dark,
Hoping for a tunnel where I could park.,
It was then, from the corner of my eye,
A shadow appeared and I gave a cry,
In panic, at the fleeting glimpse of doom,
I thought some monster stalked me in the storm,
Adrenaline coursed through me in more fright;
Then, clouds parted to let shine full moon's light.
When the monster's shadow reflected down
On an ice floe; . . . I saw it was my own.

LAP STAR

The souped-up engine reving
And exhaust ports flaming fire,
His sports car took off flying;
A squeegee squeal from each tire.

Hugging the inner oval,
Down the stretch run in a flash;
With his pit crew's approval,
Foot down, all out forward dash.

A mistake on the last curve
Was paid for in going wide.
While he corrected the swerve,
Number ten passed him inside.

He drafted behind the lead,
Trying for a winning pace;
In last moment burst of speed,
Crossed the line in second place.

WIN AND LOSE

As one, the whole house held its breath,
To win or lose, was on the line;
It could be end of sudden death,
The last-second shot was airborne.

The short arc ball failed to go in
And the crowd yelled a mighty groan.
Though saddened by what might have been,
The losers knew the margin thin.

Already thinking next season,
Sang; "wait 'til next year", with a grin.
The winners grasped the lucky win,
And took the trophy home again.

RUNNING

Astride his steed of steel,
Racing the morning sun.
To feed with toe and heel,
Riding on, 'til day is done.

Running away from world
Cares and daily demands,
Or perhaps from himself;
Yet, he tries the trail again.

He finds it not, the quest
For peace of mind within,
He seeks, he sees amiss;
It's to brave life, not to run.

Listens not to counsel,
Or whispers of conscience,
Nor truths from the Bible;
Running on, is his defense.

Astride his steed of steel,
Racing the morning sun.
To feed with toe and heel,
Riding on, 'til day is done.

SUMMERTIME HAIR

When the raindrops fall
I don't mind it at all,
Nor when birds pass the day
Scratching in my toupee;
But, what gets me down,
And raises a big frown,
Is sunshine burning red
On top of my bald head.

CLEAN KING

He sprayed all door knobs with bio jet
And mouthpiece of telephone handset.
He always used that trusty spray can,
His necessary protection plan.

He picked up lint off chairs and table,
Fluff just made him uncomfortable.
He would wipe each spot with care and frown
Those times he placed any object down.

This fussy man so afraid of germs;
With status quo, could not come to terms.
Whenever he stowed something away,
Checked and checked if it would stay.

Nervously, he'd sort over again,
The same papers, 'til sure they'll remain.
His demeanor, though not calm to me,
Taught me to take all strains serenely.

PICK YOUR SPOT

Toes pushed forward
As heels clicked hard,
Fear powered the flight
Following first fright.

I ran away
For other day;
It's not cowardly
To choose your battle.

I'll run the night
Then I will fight,
Courage I'll borrow
To fight tomorrow.

Marilynn A. Conner

CONQUEROR

A bird has sharper eyes than me and you
And sees small seeds we cannot ever view.
His tweezers can grasp the tiniest mite
And all the abundant food within sight.

He lives in rent-free homes on many hills
And pays no electric or water bills.
Richly endowed with warm coats of feather,
He'll sit on branches in any weather.

Unknown mysterious abilities
Allows traveling to far off countries.
His built-in navigation system can,
Unerringly, return him home again.

Guardedly he hops, quick as any fly,
Then, with flying swoops, soars high in the sky.
Tipping his wings in salute to the winds,
He's master of worlds where man just begins.

SMILE POWER

Greeted with a proffered smile,
Gracious, as I approached,
Destroyed my sad, somber thoughts,
And harbored, resenting mood.

Forgetting selfish anger,
I instinctively flashed back
A smile to that kind stranger;
Brighter was the day for that.

LIFE'S TRAVEL FUN

Is it the road or journey
That makes joyful trips so fun?
Or, could it be the result;
Reaching our destination?

The age-old arguments sound
Of men's diverse opinions;
If a goal is not yet found,
Can treks give satisfactions?

Progress teaches each advance
Will only come with step one;
And each great important chance,
Roads that take us to the end.

We won't recall goal's details
On paths of the past we look,
But, when life's time near fulfills,
We remember trips we took.

SENSE OF MEANINGS

RICH soil is teeming with enzymes and minerals,
For growing lush crops and vegetables;
So RICH can also apply to a man of wealth,
Or owning a business of success and health.

Just to journal English words of double meanings
Is near impossible task of listings;
To discover nuances of ideas complete,
Would probably take years to accomplish the feat.

For any mind to calculate every usage,
Is exercise in the English language,
That briefly perks interest and stimulation,
But, in the end, lasts only a generation!

SWEET DREAMS

Dreams are hard to analyze,
Like the one I dreamed last night;
Not recalled, will tantalize,
Til I give up and forget.

When nightmares scare me awake,
I remember each dark shape;
But, it's those which visions make,
Glad dreams, I won't escape.

Most nights, I don't dream at all,
Or have one that remains real;
But, there are some I recall,
Are short and sweet and ideal.

THE MEAL

The wild bunny lifted his ears straight,
Watching me closely with one eye;
Then, flicking legs as if to state
He was ready, soon, to run on by.

Every day, I'd see him scamper,
Through grass and bushes, too,
Until caught beneath my camper
And ending up in my rabbit stew.

"TO BE CONTINUED"

I remember, when growing up,
Grandpa would tell things as boy he did;
Then, Grandma called to interrupt
And Gramps would stop and say,

> "to be continued"

As lad list'ning to the radio,
Story exciting, I was engrossed,
And watched the dial of orange glow,
Until announcer said,

> "to be continued"

Time passed and television came,
With the miniseries invented;
Just when we got to know the names,.
Suspense was cut by words,

> "to be continued"

Now I'm older and life's passing;
Jesus as Savior I have received;
He paid on the cross for my sin;
When life is done, God says,

> "to be continued"

QUICKER THAN THE EYE

Those glib, fast-talking men,
Spark the target pigeons
To get emotions high,
So to bite on the deal
And ignore common sense.

For each con there's a dupe,
"A fool born per minute";
Sober headed and good
Men, but, lacking counsel,
Will find their dollars lost.

WICKED TRAIL

I climbed the hill to have a look
At the vale on the other side,
But then, I fell into near brook
And tumbled down a muddy slide.

To my rescue came a stout tree
Which I grabbed with my arms and legs
And wrapped its long limbs around me
As I scaled slope's slippery ridge.

The lesson learned on that wet day,
Don't hike the wild without a friend.
Take a companion on the way
So there's someone to lend a hand.

DELIVERY

Yoo hoo!

No answer came.
Is no one home?

Yoo hoo!

It was the same.
Should I have come?

Yoo hoo!

Could be in back?
No sound of gate.

Yoo hoo!

Put down my sack.
So ends my wait.

TO THE RESCUE

Myths of men arise from dread
And may soothe his fears on earth,
But, there's God's power instead,
To ease life of home and hearth.

Men weave stories to explain,
Fancy tales to replace God,
While they leap chasms in their brain
And each real space of His world.

They rebel against God's will,
Deep in their inner being,
Stiffened in unbelief still,
With many lost agreeing.

To the rescue is God's word,
With man's built-in common sense,
To let humans stride forward
And view myths as childishness.

WHAT IS SO BRIGHT?

What is so bright,
As a friendly smile?
It will lift your way,
And change your night
Into shining day.

What is so gray,
As a turned down frown,
Or grin, absent grace,
It'll leave, that way,
Crease lines on the face.

A friendly smile,
Is so very bright;
It will lift your way,
And change your night
into shining day.

THE BABE IN THE CRADLE

We see a babe, in a cradle,
Lord of all worlds, the King of Kings;
None could keep Him in the stable,
His work involved more than Earth's things.

We see a babe, in a cradle,
God of all, He counted it loss;
He'd not remain in the stable,
But, hung alone upon the cross.

He called himself the son of man,
He came to be like you and me;
Born to shed His blood for our sin,
And dying, paid our penalty.

It's up to us, now to believe,
To let Him Lord and Savior be;
Not by works, but by faith receive,
For by His Word, we are set free.

We see a babe in a cradle,
The God of glory born as man;
Giving to sinful world's table,
His holiness to us for Heaven.

ONWARD

The up and down slopes of stress
On our rocky trail ahead
Leaks sidetrack places of lure
Gilded byways, smooth and broad.

But, I must stay on the course
Past obstacle, cold gray clime
And uncertain future toil;
I can but venture onward.

My choice is resist pressure,
Or cave, to seek softer ways,
I then find my will stronger
By exercise 'gainst each cord.

Those powers test my resolve
And would block the road ahead,
But each step, its own reward,
A piece of the goal; onward.

ENDEAVOUR

Like a beautiful lady festooned in lacy ballroom finery,
The three masted galleon in full sail was at parade,
Sailing out on the high seas on a calm and cloudless day.

Its destination, the Pacific world of land, flora and fauna.
Discovery and sample proofs, its manifest charge
And the Orient opened to a new century, its end.

LONG TAILS

Coat tails follow where the wearer goes,
And get squashed when sat upon;
Sometimes, caught in jambs of doors,
Or, maybe ripped when a dog clamps on.

Jugglers once wore bells on each tail end;
But, since coats were made flannels,
Swallow tails fell from fashion;
Now replaced by short, squared-off panels.

Without coats, history isn't written:
From Joseph's colored coat scorned,
And cohorts of Napoleon,
To George Washington's dress uniform.

Coats from Nelson and Trafalger Square,
To John Paul Jones and his flair,
Or MacArthur's march ashore,
Historic coats have always been there.

Red coats or blue coats in future days,
Styles worn on the timeless stage,
Will reflect mysterious ways,
Of projected change in coming age.

MYSTERIES HEARD

Music of the insect world,
Sourced when wings and legs unfold,
In bow and saw-like fashion;
Night sounds of cadence action.

Comfort in cacophony,
On a quiet evening;
When in summer, I hear,
Singing clicks, bedtime is near.

The crickets chirp songs below,
And katydid strums its bow,
Some creature's sounds are muted,
My favorites, sense suited.

Many chirps may not be loud,
But, heard in a busy crowd,
Courting sounds amid the noise,
Give us relaxed airs of joys.

We learn to see with each ear,
Making invisible, clear;
We'll then find our happiness,
Hearing the mysterious.

SEARCHING

You can message me online;
If mail is returned to you,
Or I don't answer my phone,
Try my social page's view.

I'm not a private person,
And can't hide my location;
Anyone can find where I am,
Each moment, 'cross the nation.

My future place is awesome,
Joining with the busy bees;
In virtual social home,
Sailing in limitless seas.

LIFE'S TREK

I roamed the hills from light of day,
To try myself and find my way.
Climbing heights and falling down low,
With each step, increasingly slow.
Little progress I seem to gain
In life's journey, time may remain;
I'm part of family and friends
And a member of God's heaven.

LIFE-TIME

A wise man sat on high hill
And gave me a word picture,
How life and fate are fulfilled
And how to see the future.

Fate has limits, you see,
Bound by past consequences.
So, our acts form a history
That surrounds fate with fences.

Time is the engine that turns
Our work and industry on.
And, as we focus and learn,
We build fates good foundation.

There's reward because you're fit.
Never give up as you go;
You'll win just when others quit.
Live, then, with no fear to know.

FUN POEMS, PART 2

TABLE OF CONTENTS

ORANGE TREE

From deep roots, through sturdy limbs,
Nourishment travels to fruit,
Midst aroma of blossoms sweet;
First green balls of rind
That yellow with time to tart
And then aged to golden meat.

Such is works of words,
Which fashioned and polished
In inspirations airing,
Ripen upon viewing;
Rewritten and edited,
Published for golden reading.

FEAR

Energy rush in my being,
As adrenaline kicked in,
Gave me a jolt as I ran
And increased my striding span.

Trigger of my flight were things
Not seen, my imagining,
In the deathly quiet night
To give my heart startling fright.

Such thoughts, foul and murderous,
Strange are things the mind conjures,
When set in an unknown zone
And we are lost and alone.

The shadow appeared to fly,
Seen from corner of my eye.
That fluttery form behind,
Was but a loose window blind.

OUTDOORS

Changing, blustery winds blow
Breezes into gusts and gales
As thunderclouds start to grow
Like flat-bottom ships at sail.

The quiet world now begins
To add to the cold, wild, ride
Low clouds of water-logged bins
That sweep the dark countryside.

Men out in the stormy air
Are pelted with sudden rain;
Wet and cold without shelter,
Joined the land, watered again.

The weather rages above,
While I'm dry in my warm nest.
I sit beside my wood stove,
Relaxed and quiet, at rest.

WORD PLAY

A thousand words I read today
Til my eyes were bleary;
Those phrases, ideas and lines,
Of other authors were not mine.

A thousand words I dreamt today,
Where clouds, white and lacy
Soared into realms unknown;
Of wondrous tales, I recall none.

A thousand words I wrote today;
They bounced around to play,
And form a great story plot
That let me see the tale I've got.

A thousand words I set today,
Page upon page, they stay,
To charm some other along
And give to each reader a song.

SMOOTH RIDES

In my walking on beach sand,
A wayward pebble or two,
Interrupts the path I planned,
To punch the sole of my shoe.

No matter the goals of pursuit,
Sometimes small details arise,
To divert the stated route
With added cost and surprise.

Watch for things that jolt or jar,
Or may bring aches to your sides;
Thus, careful plans take you far,
Along the path of smooth rides.

IN THE WILD

I am here without much food,
And lost somewhere on my trek;
My shelter in piney wood,
Leaks water down my neck.

I tried to search boughs on high,
Through lofty trees like a scout,
To find a patch of North sky,
And a guide for my way out.

The wind has replaced the rain,
Giving me the chance to run;
The storm has moved on again,
My escape has now begun.

In battling wild nature's maze,
I found Earth's inspiration;
Adding to my breathless daze,
Exhilarating passion.

Warm and cozy in my home,
I can relax and savor,
Country trails that I had roamed,
And charm of nature's favor.

LIFE'S TRAIL

A blue smoky mist enfolds
The hills like dust cover cloths.
Greenery is turned purple
As evening meets the haze
And my light mood starts to fade.

Soon, the golden orb rises,
Soothing balm to my spirit.
Orange light to brighten my view
Where I see hope and find grit
To press on the way, anew.

Life is precious, I know,
Valuable for me and you.
Then, what I do for others,
Enriching their lives, records
My worth in great many worlds.

ON PARK'S PATH

I hiked the steep climb alone,
To clear paths of fallen stone.
To make the way easier,
And our mountain trail freer.

Ice and snow of winter time,
Brought rocky debris and grime;
And left the task of cleaning,
To Us, this and every Spring.

As volunteers, we followed,
The club's work plan as entered;
When the Summer's exercise,
Comes to each city's franchise.

Fund raising for charity,
Starts with marathon entry;
For individuals race,
In self-sacrificing pace.

The brisk air and rosy cheek,
Enliven each as they seek,
To add love to aid and care,
For the needy ones this year.

RELIABLE ACTION

To grow in character, someone has said,
Is like morning chore of making your bed.

Faced with a task you may dislike a lot,
To get it done, just give it all you've got.

Extra benefits come when you're ready,
For bigger jobs that were thought too heavy,

And sense of accomplishment you will know,
Adds confidence in life-steps as you grow.

So, whenever there is a work you dread,
Remember, always, you must make your bed.

HIGH SCALE

Many poems have been penned
Of stout men perched on steep heights;
For the top they've determined,
Is to be their climbing rights.

Inch by inch with spike and rope,
Hand o'er hand, up shear faces,
To beat the sun is the hope,
And reach the crest's high places.

In the atmosphere of stars,
Looking down from far above,
Rewards all their sweat and scars;
With great sights, always to love.

WIND POWER

The whirl of a whirlwind
Caught me by surprise,
Pushed me on my back,
And threw me to the ground.

Spun around off balance,
After I got up;
Near to fall again,
Til I tried a new stance.

This time I was ready,
In wider apart,
Solid, planted feet,
To hold, strong and steady.

But, I learned new lessons,
When facing power
Greater than I am;
Seek stronger positions.

EAR TEST

A tone will change to whistle,
If you can squeeze it real hard,
Like wind blowing in a gale,
And whipping past wet halyard,

I hear high-pitched sounding flail,
Cold air singing on taut lines;
I'm soon to quit and turn tail,
So unsettled by storm's signs.

Thuds and creaks make uncertain,
My move to escape the wind;
Which, more and more, seems to gain,
Before this voyage can end.

Now, the screaming in my ears,
And blowing sounds much louder,
I'll pull up the sea anchors,
And head for quiet harbor.

DAILY WALK

Most men take paths heavily traveled,
Those easy ways, smooth and worn.
But, some, with difficulties tackled,
Forge new trails to earn victories won.

Thus, there are many who only know
What they are told to believe.
Results recorded in history,
Are repeated in shamed mockery.

In life, mercy is sorely needed,
As we all sail fitful seas,
With unthinking sheep, never yielded
To Wisdom's kind leading into peace.

So, may you reflect on usefulness
Toward your fellow man's needs, now,
And receive the joy of helpfulness,
To allow the purest love to flow.

Traveling this orb in'time, fleeting,
Means we can help our neighbor,
Sharing love that others are seeking.
Thus, our daily walk will show we care.

COLD HIGH WINDS

North winds blew in from the sea,
Circling over desert sand;
With a changed humidity,
Warming up the low coast land.

Boisterous waves signaled storm,
As winds stirred up monstrous seas;
I hunkered down at the helm,
To ride sail 'til high winds cease.

Once again, I am at rest,
Helping my calmness restore;
Thoughts came to me that it's best,
To be home and stay ashore.

PEER PRESSURE

When being ambitious, we often find,
A new facade leaves our true self behind;
Discovering two forces in our mind,
One, the ham and second, the sober kind.

We know a little clown grows inside us,
Acting out feelings impetuously,
Yet, we must limit being too foolish,
For we might flair inappropriately.

Still, as we tug on our character's flow,
We accept behaviors we truly know.
So, pleasing men is not our way to go,
We'll be ourselves, not the other fellow.

THE GOOD NAME

Some reflect on their inherited name,
And seek to preserve its reputation;
To honor and enhance personal fame,
In respect for their ancestors station.

But, others, because of avarice and greed,
Seek selfish ends without moral compass.
Lack of guide or sense of another's need,
Leads to their good name covered with tarnish.

Day after day, we must make right choices;
Self assured to gain life that's trustworthy,
We'll hear not the rabble-rouser voices,
For clear conscience is character glory.

LOST MELODY

A song resounded in my mind,
Soft haunting air that would not leave;
Again, again, it came around,
Strange tune that continued to cleave.

Though I switched to some other song,
Hoping that cadence I'd forget,
That gripping music stayed on long,
Without a sign I could stop it.

Reminding me of waves at sea,
Returning white crests back and forth,
So that familiar melody,
Captured my head with ghostly worth.

Strange, now I think of its passing,
And remember its hold on me;
Beyond my deepest recalling,
Ever lost in my memory.

TROUBADOURS

Troubadours of the olden times,
Roamed over the rough country trails;
Singing tales and stories in rhymes,
To lift boredom with dreams and thrills.

News spread to neighboring villages,
Which sent envoys to music men,
'Visit us' said their messages,
While they set a welcoming plan.

Citizens sparking humdrum lives,
With a spirit of festival,
Like children with wide open eyes,
Waited music men's arrival.

Thus, known in the annuls of yore,
Stories of nomad pioneers,
Entertaining in song and more;
Yet today, still heard through the years.

ONE DAY

One step, one moment, one day, '
Time is fast passing away,
We march to infinity,
On this, our mortal journey.

Rolling through the universe,
Time cannot set to reverse,
So, we are destined to age,
Yet, oddly, count its passage.

One day, as we breathe our last,
We will leave this worldly past;
When our time will be no more,
And rest on a timeless shore.

TIME WARP

A star among stars shines bright
In far reaches of the universe.
We view its flickering light
Years past start of its traverse;
Sun's rays long reach into the future.

Time for living passes fast.
Life must end as it began, we see
And find each moment's soon past.
Time flees in eternity;
Mystery of growth in fleeting time.

Now, time and space enfolds me,
My journey's not a measure of miles.
Time is what it is to be;
Not for storing up in piles,
But to be used wisely every day.

PERCEPTION

The wild wolf cries to the sky,
Mournful howl from mountain high;
Sets my mood in reverie,
Of sad times in memory.

The lone wolf sings in moonlight,
A lighter tone on slopes height;
Now, that force of bright spirit,
Gives joyous outlook with it.

My attitude and thought blends,
To frequency the wolf sends;
Some far out vibration sensed,
Decreed by odd life's sentence.

LIFE'S DIVIDE

The battle is fought inside of us,
Relationships with others versus
Our aim to be individual.
Standing alone as self-sufficient
Or fellowship need to be social.

We can sit around life's group campfire,
For council and camaraderie
And sup together with friends and kin.
Or, often dream and plan on our own
And sit alone in meditation.

Both sides make our life a complete one,
Rewards and successes there to own
Into each part, our hearts seem to flow
One way, we're satisfied when alone,
But, love shared with others makes us glow.

Come, we can cease this battle of life,
For our own Id we need not deny,
While we give others our very self
And can be ourselves in life's journey;
Each, together, makes a family.

A NEW START

The empty mug
Contains the dregs
Of long past slug
With scrambled eggs.

The drink repast
Was nursed along
At days breakfast
Like a soft song.

An empty life,
Then bleeding red
Was full of strife,
But, now is dead.

Forgiveness stands,
Banning sorrows,
When self demands
Have crowned egos.

The meal complete,
Over and done.
We now have peace
As love grows on.

EGO'S DEAD END

Under veil of human trial,
A driving force of survival,
Lies the source of human ego;
This world's pride of life undertow.

When men take unobstructed chance
To seize the moment to advance,
Whether it's by stealth or deceit,
Or thievery, their goal to meet.

Without guidance of moral star,
Many have lost compass and anchor;
Their examples, how not to live,
Serve to show our love is to give.

GREAT LOVE

The world runs dry,
No milk of human kindness,
My heart does cry
For a little common sense.
Many ask; why
Is there so much selfishness?
Others will try
To salve their consciences;
The check does fly,
But where is personal-ness?
Grateful am I
To find those who give themselves,
So by and by,
For needy souls, make differences
And ne'er run dry.

A COUNTRY CHRISTMAS

I've traveled the USA
From the East to Alaska;
My best time along the way
Is Christmas in Nebraska.

     I'll sing a country Christmas,
     A country Christmas, to you.

A Christmas of warmth and joy
And a fun filled holiday,
Brings a song from this farm boy.
A country Christmas, today.

     I'll sing a country Christmas,
     A country Christmas, to you.

Come, Christmas in the country,
Out on that snow covered plain,
It's Nativity's story
And country Christmas, again.

     I'll sing a country Christmas,
     A country Christmas, to you.

Lord Jesus is the reason,
The greatest gift of ages,
We sing of joy this season;
A merry country Christmas,

I'll sing a country Christmas,
A country Christmas,
A country Christmas, to you.

MARCH TO VICTORY

Young marching men stride along
The high trail, in cadence strong.
Soon to face the enemy,
In resolute destiny;
A test of strength and mettle
To end the final battle.

In the stead of fellow men,
Brave and courageous friends,
Bound to serve the best they can;
Their utmost to the last man,
To fight against tyranny
And gain precious victory.

STANDARD OF LOYALTY

Waving flag upon far hill
Marks my country's glory, still.
Born out of brave patriots' valor
Our banner of courage and honor.

The climb up the hill of life
Is filled with struggles and strife,
And makes us grateful for their bravery
And our given opportunity.

From the top of ev'ry hill,
Each view of future's dim veil
Confirms our journey of victory
When we conquer our place on the way.

Now, that flag still waves on high,
To carry us 'til we die.
Though, for us, it is a difficult fight,
Our flag of hope keeps us through the night.

Ready to the last man's breath,
Face to face, a date with death;
From minutemen to special ops,
They are standing in the gap for us.

Waving flag upon the hill,
Marks my country's glory, still.
Born out of brave patriots' valor;
Our banner of courage and honor.

YAW AND PITCH OF LIFE

The ship bobbed up and down,
Like a cork in a bowl,
Lacking crew, went aground;
No witness, not a soul.

I know this, because you see,
I was thrown out on land,
As the storm swept me free,
And launched all on the sand.

Rescued, I now reviewed,
Trust of dangerous seas;
How mankind sails anew,
Lured by oceans he sees.

A vessel needed crew,
I signed on the voyage;
For the captain I knew,
And I'll turn life's new page.

SAILORS

Our vessel ventured far in time,
Out from ocean beach,
Into dark realm of the mistress,
Vast and roiling sea;
Yet, we shall sail on.

We're bound by fish and bird domain,
Where wayward wind sweeps
And storm's force can tear from surface,
Down to the black deeps;
Yet, we can sail on.

Wet sting of boisterous water,
Threatens our voyage,
As we ply our strange path, without
A near land refuge;
Yet, we will sail on.

May we board the faithful Pilot,
Guide for soul comfort,
And so complete our journey sweet,
Safe in heaven's port;
And, never sail on.

CARILLON BELLS

In seeking rest from fast paced walk,
We found a bench where we could talk,
In sunshine touched garden bower,
Beneath the carillon tower.

The bells' sounds came to us below,
Wafted music, like long ago,
When once, friend Ron had let us sit
In tight, cramped space of belfry pit.

His quick, skilled moves on each lever,
Made sweet bell notes still remembered
Music that brings us back again,
We'll enjoy in hours that remain.

MERRY CHRISTMAS

With frosty wings we fly,
Through snowy clouds on high,
And land on the green plain
Of famous Christmas Mountain.

The message, crystal clear,
In bright displays appear;
Jesus came as Savior,
To conquer sin, forever.

His love for us brought Him
The cross from Bethlehem;
"Merry Christmas" we say,
To honor Him Christmas Day.

We observe Jesus' birth,
God's visit time to earth,
But, forget "holiday",
We celebrate Christmas Day.

RESIDUALS

We can wipe the slate clean, yet
Some dust will be left behind.
We can forgive and forget,
But, consequences remain.

We can set the record straight,
But, we're to be the payor
For getting on the road right
And our repairs of error.

Our actions cause reactions,
'Tis the fact of life and true.
Lesson learned by all factions:
Just own up for what we do.

WHITE PASTE

In my memory.

The town roust-a-bout, Willie Will,
At many odd jobs, worked downtown
Washing storefront window and sill.

We boys found great fascination
Watching him paste ads with his skill
Brush flying on the billboard sign.

Willie worked as freelancers will
And lived his life in freedom fine.
Sounds of his whistle remain still;

In my memory.

TO BE FORGOTTEN

He planned to retire in April,
But, said it was unofficial
And for me to keep it quiet
Until such time he announced it.

There may be a little sadness
When I reflect the future days,
At our place, after he has gone
And left his desk sitting alone.

Life will go on, as living must,
And we grow emotional crust;
Losing ourselves in continuing
Daily plots among the living.

SIDE TRACKS

Needed steps of life
              get in our way,
Detours to prevent
              apt silent times.
Too fast we go to
              discover within,
Deeper values of
              joy and meaning;
Or, no time to search
              purpose of life
And look into our
              soul's inner self.
Oh, that we would just
              meditate more,
Then, be able to
              live full and true.

PASSING TIME

I rose at dawn to a fresh day,
Greeting new opportunities,
With restored vigor to display,
And conquer all worldly duties.

Noon rushes by and tasks are done,
With chores piled up to fill the slate;
Laboring sweat beneath the sun,
Foreshadows fading daylight's fate.

Twilight warns our time is passing,
And early darkness soon to turn,
Into black of night, unending;
As time expires, our day is done.

When we see a new day dawning,
Wrapped up in duties until noon;
We forget at each fresh morning,
Our daytime will set all too soon.

TWIN TOWERS AMBUSH

Ten thousand souls were there that day,
The targets of unkown demons.
Some escaped the crash and flames,
But, we still mourn horrible deaths
Of innocents in the path of hate
And honor those who stood in the gap
The trapped to rescue and to save.

Two buildings are down in ashy heaps,
But, onward do our hearts traverse
The sorrow and waste we feel,
To resolve to fight cowardly hate;
Steadfastly to defend our country.
For patriot heroes and the free—
We remember—God knows and sees.

VICTORY

Somber thought sets the mood,
As darker rain clouds loom,
And I stay in my room,
Fighting shadows of gloom.

I can't yield to despair,
Or succumb to old fear;
God has promised to bear,
My load by His power.

Look, I see the sunrise,
And with grateful voice raise,
To God, who brings bright skies,
Prayers of thanks and praise.

MOVING SEA OF TIME

Plying waters of sea,
Is joyous heaven to me;
Stiff wind and billowed sail,
Excites my soul without fail.

I sail through salt spray air,
With blow and wave to conquer;
Buoyed in sea's abundance,
There's no limits and no fence.

The ocean beckons me,
To savor its liberty;
I sail on in freedom,
And enjoy God's creation.

Voyages are over,
Time has anchored me ashore;
There my skiff lays empty,
Yet, I yearn to sail wild sea.

THE TRIP

On the way to the sea,
I wondered what was ahead for me;
Thrust upon a journey
I had not chosen it to be.

A path which to follow,
Worlds I need to learn and know,
The ways and means to grow
And guide me where my star will go.

Can't wait for tomorrow,
But, knowledge must be added now.
No evolutions vow,
Today, do real options allow.

On my way is the toll
I've paid for the passage in full.
Old road reach seems so small,
Too soon, the end becomes the call.

SAID THE RECTOR

Somewhere in this sanctuary,
I think we had a robbery,
The Rector said to me.

Someone took the offertory
Fund, but how, is the mystery,
The Rector said to me.

You come with famed reputation
And we depend on discretion,
The Rector said to me.

It's urgent we've a solution,
Please solve the fund location,
The Rector said to me.

Opening the jammed drawers you found,
Revealed the benevolent fund,
The Rector said to me.

Gratitude has many layers,
God, through you, has answered prayers,
The Rector said to me.

We'll know who stuck the fund away,
When he tries to get it today,
The Rector said to me.

CLASS

Ssh, ssh, shoeshine man,
Swish, swish, soap sponge dish.
Dab, dab, dark dye can,
Brush, brush, buffed finish.
Slap, slap, soft cloth shine,
Ah, ah, high art polish;
Step/step, sharp showman.

BLIND EYES

I once knew a gal who liked to fly,
Ten feet off the ground, head in the sky
There was no job too big, or too small.
She was busy from the Spring to Fall.

She was a helper to all who cried
And would finish work others had tried.
She continued help even when ill,
Strangely, only few had thanks to tell.

Now came the time when she was in need,
'Tis sad tale of life, many don't heed.
And though she helped them in their crisis,
Few did come to her side to assist.

THE PRESENT

The sign of the hour of three,
When what's gone before is seen
And future is yet to be,
Is the middle of life's scene.

Promise and time to achieve,
The present, our precious gift.
If we will only believe,
Our souls and spirits can lift.

Remember the hour of three,
Then, give up the past as spent;
Forget what's going to be;
Live the now, and be content.

MYSTERIES PROFOUND

Could a shadow be without light?
Can light shine if there's no darkness?
Can vast oceans breath without waves?
Waves ebb and flow without the seas?
Can time be without the living?
Or life lived without moving time?
There are those who love pat answers,
Only show what little they know.
They are like wild erratic winds,
Haunting us with changing theories.

EAGLE

Rare, the sight of an eagle asleep,
But, monitors his world from on high,
Alert, in far surveillance to keep;
And aloft, on massive wings does fly.

Majestic sweep of feathers, sunlit,
Gives him an awesome look of power,
Inspiring men to set no limit
To their aim of courage and honor.

NATURE'S RUN

Looking down from my perch on Flat Rock,
On the misty valley stretched below;
I could make out the big tower clock,
And county courthouse covered with snow.

Lights flickered like far shimmering stars,
As I watched autos buck the weather.
On roads, snowplows gouged out winding scars,
And each tree's snow became a feather.

The morning hours passed by so quickly,
I barely had time to stoke the fire,
And start my chores that came up weekly,
So I'd end before time to retire.

There are more places I need to go,
More agendas and papers to write;
Then, perhaps, I will finally know
—When the end is faced and I reach night.

MYSTERY FORM

A dark shadow formed in the night;
Out of mist and cloud, it loomed
In purple gray sea of moonlight,
Moving, silent sign of doom.

Near, but far, the weird sound of horn
Travels with wavering wind,
In hollow reverberation,
To echo majestic sound.

Advancing, 'tis the giant form
Of growling monster, awheel,
And with noise of clattering drum
Becomes shape of Diesel steel.

ROBOT HERO

The most famous robot of ages,
With the name of number Six-Oh-Gee,
Had his story written on pages
Of science books and space history.

How he was so famous, you can see,
For he flew his ion ship into space
And saved all earth men great misery,
When he zapped alien germ pods away.

Now don't tell me that is just sci-fi,
And that is a fictional story;
I come from far space to testify,
This is from your future history.

FREEDOM'S FLAG

Rolling through the flag, a gentle zephyr,
Brings to it a steady, moving salute,
With rippling waves that slowly wander,
Over the field of the red, white and blue.

Wind waves slowly move throughout old glory,
Undulating in artistic motion,
Lifting my spirit with patriots' story,
And filling my heart with high emotion.

I shall proudly stand by the flag unfurled,
The symbol of liberty and freedom,
Over all the international world;
America, opportunity's home.

WARM HEART

Within, without, winter breeze
Covers me with frigid air.
My fingers begin to freeze,
For I have no gloves to wear.

How suddenly the warm winds,
Died away in the last hour;
Then, thoughts of south sea islands,
Come as cold blasts gain power.

Like problems that rise in life,
And are soon destined to end,
In midst of sad and cold strife,
There's a day, warmth comes again.

HARD LIFE

Alas, the steps seem so steep;
I must scale the soaring slope.
Then, I know the key to keep
Before I have half a hope;
That is reach and dig down deep,
To fight and stay selfish scope,
And sail on successes sweep.

QUIET HERO

He crept along the wall,
Grabbing at a hanging vine;
Every few steps he'd fall,
Slipping down grassy incline.

In each soft quiet step,
He slowly approached unheard,
Searchlight dodged as it swept,
Til he made it to the ford.

There, a musty mulch stench
In dark cover of trees,
Joined sweet flowery scents,
To let his mind be at ease.

Sharp, and with watchful eye,
He reached hostage prison shed,
Freeing them in glad cry,
Joining the crowd as they fled.

His goal he sought to find
When he quickly led the way:
Leave vile vestige behind
Of tyranny's grasp that day.

So he became a hero,
And subject of famous song;
Attempts to find him, zero,
He was humble, free and gone.

GROWING

Ivy climbs upon my wall,
—Growing, growing, high and tall.
Though I prune it to the ground,
It grows again with a bound.

Green and beautiful, in place,
Will change and extend its chase
And conquer with jungle sleeves,
Til my wall becomes all leaves.

As we live, ivy tells me,
High and tall is growth to be;
To complete our life's true wall
And fulfill destiny's call.

SE LA VIDA

Pablo saw the shiny craft
With tall mast and shallow draft
There hard tied, snug in her slip,
And yearned for that little ship.

With the owner did prevail
And so bought his dream vessel;
Readies it with emotion,
To get set for the ocean.

Prepped to paint became a chore
To keep him anchored ashore.
In a huff, he works away,
To lose each good sailing day.

Caulked and painted, it looks bright
Ready for a sail tonight.
But, fast moving storm and gale
Keeps him from his first sail

Pablo felt he's now in scrapes,
Caught by conflicting escapes.
So, for ease of mind and toil,
His "La Vida" is on sale.

ON THE WALL

We know mankind's trait of wall fetish,
Which borders on worship of idols,
Because people won't stop or finish,
Practice of putting their lives on walls.

Near each gate hangs an enameled sign,
'Keep Out' is one message it may send,
Advertisements do some walls contain,
Encouraging consumers to spend.

Some are painted political friezes;
To change viewers subliminally.
And murals show picture messages,
For citizens to note visually.

Colorful walls of ceramic tiles,
Displayed from ancient's excavations,
Of tomb walls facia or church temples,
That enhance their beautifications.

How we use our walls reveals culture,
Like ceramic tiles of history;
What is seen on walls of our future,
Will rest on technology's story.

MASQUERADE

Darkness slowly creeps into our land,
Perhaps unnoticed by common man,
Diming virtue and good behavior;
Turning morality off-color.

There is a switch of counter culture;
What was once society proper
Standing up against moral evils,
It's culture attacking good morals.

How did this upside down mess occur?
While we watched society's structure;
It's when we let down our guard within
The counter culture came dancing in.

A NEW LIFE

I hummed a tune, hoping my hurt to ease,
But my grief and sorrow would not cease;
And like the lost song of a skylark,
Became only a whistle in the dark.

This story will go on 'til end of time,
As recorded in bards of old rhyme
And in sad voices of our forbears,
Reminding us it'll go on through our years.

Now I go on, a snip of memory
Or thought of what we had together,
Each to stab my heart with loss again;
But, her memory honored, despite pain.

When we think of her unselfish service,
Always ever loving and joyous;
Giving her best for little reward
Is how in life she earned such high regard.

She knew God promised a home in heaven
To everyone who believes in Him,
And who takes Him as Savior and Lord;
For He cut every sin and sadness cord.

WARM SONG

Do you remember a quiet summer eve?
Breeze flowing enough to show a world alive
As a background sound of a loon's mourning call,
And other worlds of living creatures tell.

In wonder, we hear soft song that doesn't cease,
And we find ourselves in such comforting peace
That the breath of sense in serene happiness
Can only be exceeded by heaven's bliss.

CAPTURED

In the wild life of ranching,
Of a worth without measure,
Is the horse, its great treasure.

A horse comes with attached strings,
Like back breaking bales of hay,
Feeding and cleaning each day.

Curry combing and rubbings;
Rewarded in grateful eyes
And contented mumbling sighs.

Making demeanor gentling;
You begin to see of course,
How magnetic is my horse;

He captures me each morning.

WAYWARD THOUGHTS OF MAN

Some call the ways of mankind,
Unexplainable and weird.
Which logic can't understand;
Here are examples I've heard:
The world is flat and you'll fall
Off the edge when you sail near,
The sun moves around the Earth
And not Earth, the orbiter.

Does egg or chicken come first
When the answer should be clear.
Does a falling tree make sounds
If no one is there to hear?
Life's determined by stars call,
Controlled by some old light-year.
Your path crossed by cat if black
Can result in bad luck. fear.

Other dire and awful things:
Bad luck walk under ladder,
Steps on cracks for a bad back,
Seven for broken mirror
God knows each man before birth,
In own eyes, man does better.
But, God's true wisdom's above,
His thoughts are heaven higher.

HIT AND OR MISS

Our muscles grow,
If used, we know;
But, we are slow,
Lest time bestow
A vibrant glow.
We run and go.

Move to and fro;
Exercised so,
Needs each day's flow.
We daily sow
To gain the show,
So we can grow.

LADY LUCK

Woman,

Who sits her steed with grace,
Who rides the wind to race;
Conquering turf and track,
Headlong to Hell and back.

Woman,

Who ready at the wire,
Who finds her heart afire;
Shod hoofs dig in to feed,
A blurred image of speed.

Woman,

Who holds boots stirrup side,
Who hugs breeches astride;
A queen's touch in her rein,
Flying on Black to win.

THE POEM I DIDN'T WRITE

There is a poem I didn't write,
Which could help no earthly soul.
Starting with ah! And ending with oh!
It contains cliches so very trite.

It was all in a tongue, archaic
And there was no need for rhyme.
I thought it so clever, at the time,
That a better I could never make!

The recipe was spiced with love,
Sprinkled in with June and Moon.
Spring noises were added to the tune
Of heart and soul and heaven above.

It dripped with sentiment divine,
Followed by a sad, sweet air.
Oh, I wish someone would only care
About that so perfect poem of mine.

No notes or reviews cause me fright;
It's verse, no friends memorize.
Ever lost on those who humanize,
That wonderful poem I didn't write!

INSIDE POETRY

One glance in a shop window
Sees but a few displays there.
On second look, items show
And appear, not seen before.

Poems describe lofty ways,
Music set to language beams.
Yet, it's lore must have replays
To reveal more deeps and dreams.

When poets share life in rhyme,
Their inner thoughts become known.
But, when read time after time,
Varied nuances are shown.

Poems need respect to live
Out the message found within.
We serve ourselves, then, to give
A fond look inside again.

UNUSUAL

He is standing tall, on stage,
Gangling thin, wide-eared boy.
Hair uncombed, spiked all over;
Singing an awesome tenor voice.

 . . . It is unusual.

So nervous about this place,
Up there, he is alone.
Many eyes fixed upon him,
But, no sign of his shaking heart.

 . . . It is unusual.

Love messages in his song
Touches everyone's soul;
Moves the audience to tears
And inspires the spirits to soar.

 . . . is unusual.

MOVED ON

The house is empty;
Every step echoes off the walls.
No furniture is seen,
Except an old wooden rocker.

The sun shines brightly,
Glaring through unshaded windows
Upon the brown varnish;
Flooring now streaked and worn by time.

The owners have moved,
Some greener pasture uptown.
Sad to leave that old home,
But excited, new to explore.

"Does the future hold,"
The owner asks, "raze or rebuild?"
Only time will tell us;
But for now, the house is empty.

SOULS IN SLAVERY

Waves relentlessly pound, sift and grind
    Sand of our short days.
Pagan culture presses to its mold
    Unheeding sheep to dreadful fate;
Coaxed to amoral webs of desire.

It attempts to blot out time itself,
    Life's vapors fleeting,
Leaving only vacuous frail space;
    Losing precious life's ownership
To bribery of false ambition.

Corral of law limits our expanse;
    Breathes its will on all,
Controlling prince and common alike.
    Preserving ponderous might by
Fleecing that feeds growth, ever more growth.

Ego and selfishness conspire to
    Join envy and pride,
Seeking one's own and not other's need,
    Using weapons that cheat and lie;
Destroying relationships and truth.

Waves relentlessly pound, sift and grind
    Sand of our short days.
Pagan culture presses to its mold
    Unheeding sheep to dreadful fate;
Coaxed to amoral webs of desire.

FUTILE APPEASEMENT

Men who march to war
Distractions do disdain
To focus face forward
And gain against the grain;
Patriots, to the core.

A few decry the fight,
Though cowardly attacked.
But it's defensive might
Used 'gainst threatening act
That saves us in the night.

Standing in the gaps;
Troops protect families,
Safe from terror traps;
By their great sacrifices,
Harm and death perhaps.

Trembling not the test,
Stand to confront the foe.
Buckler and battle best,
Men of selfless ego,
Brave beyond the highest.

COUNT DOWN TO THE END

Two outs and down in the count,
I must make the most of the play;
Pitches beginning to mount,
I need to make contact to stay.

How long can I go before
I'm gone at the game's last inning?
We don't have a chance to score,
If I miss and go down swinging

I'm standing and watching in
Sadness and sorrow of lost game,
Using hours that are left me
Til I've reached the end of the time.

Yet, I see a door open
Before my spiritual eyes,
Where there is life, without end,
In the loving arms of Jesus.

BEACON OF AMERICA

I walk ways of life in America, I see freedom,
I know hope for the future, and I find love for today.

I see in our patriot's symbol;
White, purity of purpose, blue, opportunity and bravery,
and red for the price it cost.

White stars that stand for a republic and a voice for me.

Proudly honored at parades, sporting events, and public
cere-monies;
It waves on high to proclaim our great nation of morals and
laws.

I stand, with goosebumps and shivers, to salute "Old Glory".